THE LITTLE LITTLE GATE-CRASHER

THE LIFE AND PHOTOS OF MACE BUGEN

BY GABRIELLE KAPLAN-MAYER

WITH A FORWARD BY MIKE SAGER

THE SAGER GROUP

Artifex Te Adiuva

Enjoy Mace's adventure!

♡, *Gabrielle*

The Little Gate-Crasher: The Life and Photos of Mace Bugen.
By Gabrielle Kaplan-Mayer

Cover designed by Stravinski Pierre and Siori Kitajima,
SF AppWorks LLC http://www.sfappworks.com
Formatting by Siori Kitajima and and Ovidiu Vlad for SF AppWorks LLC
E-book formatted by Ovidiu Vlad

Cataloging-in-Publication data for this book
is available from the Library of Congress.

ISBN-13: 978-0-9964901-4-6
ISBN-10: 0-9964901-4-0

Published by The Sager Group LLC
info@TheSagerGroup.net

Photos Courtesy Lynn Auerbach-Kaplan
Scanning by North Shores Printery, Pacific Beach, CA

THE LITTLE
GATE-CRASHER

THE LIFE AND PHOTOS OF
MACE BUGEN

**BY GABRIELLE
KAPLAN-MAYER**

**WITH A FORWARD
BY MIKE SAGER**

For My Mom,
Lynn Auerbach-Kaplan

Moishe Morris "Mace" Bugen
June 12, 1915 – October 31, 1982

Mace Bugen might have been an achondroplastic dwarf—43 inches tall with an average size head and torso set on small, twisted legs—but that didn't mean he was an idiot or a pushover. In truth, he was smarter than most; over the years, he learned to effectively turn what society in those days called a *handicap* into a powerful tool he could use to his advantage.

"When I was a kid," he once said, "I'd ask myself, *Why is that guy on the football team? Why can't I be on the team? Why didn't God give me the height so I could be the hero?*

"Then at some point I figured it out: I gotta do something special to let 'em know I'm me."

LIST OF PHOTOS

PAGE 10. With Joe Louis. Nicknamed "The Brown Bomber," Louis held the world heavyweight championship from 1937–1949. He was Bugen's first celebrity acquaintance.

PAGE 11. With "Jersey Joe" Walcott. A New Jersey–born fighter, Walcott broke the world's record for the oldest man to win the heavyweight title at age 37. In 1965, he refereed the controversial world heavyweight championship bout between Muhammad Ali and Sonny Liston.

PAGE 14. Mace in his "Hadassah" Jeep. "I never got mad at God. I figured he made me so that's it," he once said.

PAGE 17. With Harry James. The big band leader, James played trumpet with Benny Goodman and later was the first to hire a young vocalist named Frank Sinatra.

PAGE 18. With Jane Russell (far right). One of Hollywood's sex symbols in the 1940s and 1950s, Russell played opposite Marilyn Monroe in *Gentlemen Prefer Blondes*. 1971.

PAGE 19. With (left to right) Burgess Meredith, Anne Jackson and Edward G. Robinson. Meredith was an actor on both stage and screen—known more recently for his roles as the Penguin in the *Batman* television series and as Sylvester Stalone's trainer in *Rocky*. Jackson was an Obie-winning, Tony-nominated stage actress. Robinson, an actor during Hollywood's Golden Age, was known for playing gangsters and was given an Honorary Academy Award after his death in 1973. 1968.

PAGE 20. With Jack Benny (right). The comedian got his start in vaudeville and radio and then transformed his TV variety show into the first sitcom.

PAGE 21. With Danny Kaye. The popular actor/singer/dancer/comedian/television personality is best remembered for playing the title characters in *The Secret Life of Walter Mitty* and *Hans Christian Anderson*. 1971.

PAGE 22. With Sammy Davis Jr. The iconic black, Jewish, and one-eyed member of the Rat Pack was a singer, dancer, actor, and beloved personality.

PAGE 23. With Isaac Stern (center). The renowned Jewish violinist played around the globe but refused to perform in Germany. He mentored younger musicians, including cellist Yo-Yo Ma and violinist Itzhak Perlman. 1976.

PAGE 24. With Jack Gilford. The Broadway actor and film star was nominated for Tony Awards for his roles in *A Funny Thing Happened On The Way To The Forum* and *Cabaret*. He was blacklisted during the McCarthy era for his social activism.

PAGE 25. With Richard Bernard "Red" Skelton. The comedic actor got his start in the early days of radio and went on to host "The Red Skelton Show" on TV for two decades. 1971.

PAGE 26. With Ella Fitzgerald. Known as "The First Lady Of Song," the jazz singer won 13 Grammy awards and sold more than 40 million albums in her lifetime. 1973.

credited for sparking the resurgence of the American conservative political movement in the 1960s.

FORWARD

Some time ago, on assignment for *Esquire* magazine, I spent several days and nights in the company of the actor Peter Dinklage, one of the stars of the popular and award-winning television series *Game of Thrones*. A gifted performer with a resonant voice, acclaimed as well for his work on the stage and the bigscreen, he is distinguished also by his dwarfism.

Walking the rainy streets of New York City with a world-famous four-foot man in a black hoodie and Chelsea boots, breakfasting in his favorite haunt, playing drunken Scrabble with his friends in a worn red leather booth until the wee hours at the historic and homey Knickerbocker Bar and Grill, I got to know him a little bit. He has a special intellect and is funny as hell, as sly and sardonic and wickedly observational as his character on *GOT*. But what stuck with me most is the way he has, over the years, turned what many in society consider to be a disability into unique sense of himself. He is a man who always wanted to be special, just not for the reasons everybody thought. Somehow, he has willed it to happen.

Mace (far right) at the bar mitzvah of Sager's uncle, Paul R. Sager.

Before meeting Dinklage, as most journalists would, I did a lot of research. Sitting at my desk at home, going through the pages and pages of articles and reviews, an odd, distracting thought began to clank around in the attic of my memory . . . a dim specter of a photograph I'd inherited from my paternal grandmother.

I did a bit of digging and unearthed it: a 4-by-2-inch photo proof from my now-deceased uncle's bar mitzvah party, held in the summer of 1954 at my grandparents' house in the Civil War town of Fredericksburg, Virginia. A group photo typical of any family occasion, this one included my great-grandfather, my great aunt's husband, a cousin of my dad's generation, and, at the very end of the row, standing on a chair, a short and crooked little man wearing a snazzy custom-tailored suit and a bow tie.

I got on the horn with my great-uncle, William "Buddy" Sager, who was ninety-four at the time, and his niece Alice Haber, who was eighty—Alice was the cousin in the photo. Both are still healthy and with us. Both have memories like steel traps. And both identified the dwarf as Moishe "Mace" Bugen. His mother was Sarah Sager Bugen, the sister of my great grandfather, Lewis "Pop" Sager, who had immigrated from Lithuania and eventually settled in the mountains of western Virgina, in the town of Front Royal, where he began as a junk monger with a horse and wagon and eventually owned several stores on the main street of town. During prohibition, the story goes, he sold glass jars out of the family's clothing store by the boxful to local moonshiners. No doubt his little service helped keep the peace during semiannual marches through the town square by hooded members of the Ku Klux Klan.

Uncle Buddy is a retired Marine major who saw intense action in the South Pacific during World War II. He would later become a high-ranking government attorney. To this day he is the family historian; in no time I found myself emailing with a distant cousin named Lynn Auerbach Kaplan. Lynn's mother, Minerva Bugen Auerbach, was Mace Bugen's sister. It turned out that Lynn's daughter, Gabrielle Kaplan-Mayer, had been working on a history of her great-uncle Mace, my distant cousin.

After a few more emails I spoke on the phone with Kaplan-Mayer. Mace, she said, had lived in Phillipsburg, New Jersey. He drove a specially equipped Jeep, not a common civilian vehicle back then, which gave him an official air. After World War II, he made a small fortune rehabbing houses and selling to returning veterans; he was well known for his charity work around town, particularly in the Jewish community. For more than thirty years, he never missed an athletic contest—baseball, football, basketball—between Phillipsburg High School and its closest rival. For twenty years, Mace was the official timekeeper for league basketball games at the Young Men's Hebrew Association—though it was well known that if the home team was losing, five minutes left on the clock could sometimes stretch to fifteen . . . nobody was going to argue with the dwarf. There is an undocumented story about the time Mace grabbed the scorer's clock and hid it somewhere down his pants. Suffice it to say he was a character and that he was well loved.

As his four siblings had kids of their own, Mace also made time for weekly dates with his seven nieces and nephews

—everyone's favorite outings were to Calliope's Sweet Shop and Rapp's Ice Cream Fountain. Likewise, Mace didn't miss a special event—if there was a bar mitzvah or a wedding going on in the vicinity, you'd find him on the guest list.

An observant Jew, Mace was a regular at the little shul in Easton, Bnai Abraham, where he went weekly to observe the Sabbath. Every December, he drove a car full of fellow shul members (besides the Jeep, he owned a specially equipped Studebaker) to New York City for the annual Hanukkah ball to benefit Israel Bonds; likewise, he patronized the annual ball in Philadelphia. As time went by, Mace would customize his Jeep with a Jewish theme, painting it blue and white, the colors of the Israeli flag, and covering the vehicle in Jewish stars. In the surrounding Lehigh Valley, where only 2 percent of the population was Jewish, Mace was like a one-man Jewish pride parade. "If you went to something—a service, a concert, any event in the Jewish community— and Mace wasn't there, you were like, 'Where's Mace?'" remembers an Easton friend from those years.

In 1946, at age thirty-one, Mace ran for the office of town commissioner of Phillipsburg. His slogan: "I'm for the Little Guy."

Though he lost the election by a wide margin, by the time it was over, everyone in the Lehigh Valley knew his name.

As he got older and less mobile, his sister Minerva constructed a spacious apartment behind her house built entirely to his scale. This was back in 1964. Kaplan-Mayer remembers playing delightedly with her siblings as a child in their great-uncle's giant dollhouse.

And one more thing, Kaplan-Mayer said.

Mace had an unusual hobby.

Kaplan-Mayer's mother was in possession of several albums of yellowed photographs Mace had left behind.

There was Mace with Joe DiMaggio. Mace with Muhammad Ali. Mace with Richard Nixon, Jonas Salk, Sammy Davis Jr., Edward G. Robinson, Jane Russell, Danny Kaye, George Gobel, Milton Berle, Jackie Mason, Tom Jones. (There is video of Mace running into a boxing ring in a famous heavyweight bout between Ezzard Charles and Joe Louis, the Brown Bomber, who liked to hang out with Mace (who had famously crashed the ring during Louis' first pro bout, kissed Louis' gloves and offered the future champ "a little Jewish luck.")

Most of the photos were taken in New York or nearby cities. In all of them, the celebs appear somewhat dazed. Clearly they'd been ambushed. Their expressions seem to say: "How could I possibly refuse?"

In a way, you could say that Mace—at a time before cell phones or Andy Warhol—was the world's first practitioner of the celebrity selfie. Or maybe you could say more accurately that he was perhaps the world's first selfie photobomber. Over a period of three decades, using his unique combination of guile, cunning, handicap, and sense of entitlement, Mace engineered photos of himself with some of the biggest celebrities of his day.

In a column dated September 28, 1955, Walter Winchell, the iconic and fedora-wearing syndicated gossip columnist, included this item in his roundup:

"The dwarf who crashes the gate at most major sports events (past the cops and attendants) is 'Mace' Bugen, an insurance and realty man of Phillipsburg, N.J."

Thereafter, Mace was dubbed the "The Little Gate-Crasher."

"When I was a kid," Mace Bugen once told Kaplan-Mayer, "I'd ask myself, 'Why is that guy on the football team? Why can't I be on the team? Why didn't God give me the height so I could be the hero?'

"Then at some point I figured it out: I gotta do something special to let 'em know I'm me."

* * *

Reading Kaplan-Mayer's fascinating portrayal of Mace Bugen, a large man in a small, twisted body, I couldn't help but be reminded of my time spent with Peter Dinklage. Maybe it was artistic license, or an undue melding of impressions and details in the caldron of my experience, but I couldn't help extrapolating a certain kindred spirit between Mace and Dink. Certainly they shared a number of qualities.

Yes, both were achondroplastic dwarfs—though Mace was considerably more twisted and appeared to be in perpetual discomfort. Dinklage has benefited considerably by the advances of modern medicine.

Both men came from families that offered unconditional love and support. Neither man labored under the notion that his affliction was anything more than a genetic fact, another of life's many obstacles to be overcome. Like the actor, Mace Bugen grew up with a sense that he wanted to be special, that he wanted to distinguish himself, that he wanted to be well known and appreciated—just not for the reasons everybody thought. Somehow, he willed it to happen.

I can see him now, Mace the local real estate kingpin, climbing down with some difficulty from his Jeep and then lowballing a startled buyer on a purchase price. Or breaching the security around President Richard Nixon. Or making his way into the Yankees' locker room to meet Joe DiMaggio. Or climbing through the ring ropes before a Joe Louis fight.

Jonas Salk, the inventor of the polio vaccine, and all the members of his party, are on their knees in their photo op with Mace, apparently to be able to pose at Mace's level. I can only imagine what transpired. Each of the photos has a similar story to tell. Unfortunately, only a handful has survived by oral tradition. These are recounted in Kaplan-Mayer's text. She was ten when Mace died. The rest must be left to the imagination.

When my evening at the Kinckerbocker with Dink turned into a friendly booze-and-Scrabble fest with a couple of his homies from Bennington College, I found the courage to pull out my bar mitzvah photo of Mace.

"Oh my," Dink exclaimed. "He's got serious issues. What's he standing on?"

"A chair," I offered.

Dink picked up the photo as if it were something diseased and looked more closely. "He should have gotten the operation on his legs. See how he's overweight and his legs are bowing? That's why my parents got my legs straightened. And that's why I go to the gym. Look at his tiny—oh God, you're still recording?"

—Mike Sager

SPORTS FIGURES

With Joe DiMaggio. The New York Yankees centerfielder, known as
"Joltin' Joe," was married to Marilyn Monroe and still holds a major
league baseball record for his a 56-game hitting streak.

With Muhammed Ali, 1970. Considered the greatest heavyweight in the history of boxing, Ali was a polarizing figure during the early part of his career due to his political outspokenness.

With Meadowlark Lemon (and boys from the Tallis & Tefillin club), 1970.
Known as the "Clown Prince" of the Harlem Globetrotters, Lemon was also
an ordained minister and TV star.

With Hank Aaron, 1972. "Hammerin' Hank" Aaron is one
of only two players to hit 30 or more home runs in a season at least
fifteen times.

With Bob Feller, 1971. An eight-time All-Star with the Cleveland Indians,
Feller was ranked 36th on *The Sporting News Selects Baseball's 100 Greatest
Players* and was named the publication's "greatest pitcher of his time."

With Mario Andretti. The naturalized US citizen was the only
race car driver to win the Indianapolis 500, Daytona 500, and the
Formula One World Championships.

With Willie Mays, 1972. The Hall of Famer started his career
in the Negro American League and went on to be named to the
Sporting News's "100 Greatest Players" list.

With Bill Russell. The All-Star center lead the Celtics to
11 NBA championships and went on to become the NBA's first
African American coach.

With Larry Holmes, 1973. At age 22, the Easton, PA,
native got his big break as a sparring partner for Muhammad Ali.
Later he would beat Ali and become heavyweight champion.

SEASON S GREETINGS AND BEST WISHES
FOR THE NEW YEAR

With Joe Louis. Nicknamed "The Brown Bomber,"
Louis held the world heavyweight championship from 1937–1949.
He was Bugen's first celebrity acquaintance.

With "Jersey Joe" Walcott. A New Jersey–born fighter, Walcott broke
the world's record for the oldest man to win the heavyweight title
at age 37. In 1965, he refereed the controversial world heavyweight
championship bout between Muhammad Ali and Sonny Liston.

INTRODUCTION

When my great-uncle Morris "Mace" Bugen died in 1982, at the age of 66, the albums of his celebrity photos were left to my grandmother Minerva, his older sister. When Minerva started suffering from dementia in the mid-1990s, we moved her into a nursing facility and sold her house. Many of her treasures, including Mace's albums, were stored in my parents' home. Often when my siblings and I were visiting my parents, we'd take out the albums and look at them and marvel at Mace's chutzpah and how he was the coolest uncle of all times. "These photos should be in a book," my mom would always say.

I agreed but never took her idea too seriously. In those days, I was busy trying to write plays and then later started writing nonfiction and educational curriculum. Life happened; Mace's photos stayed frozen in time. When I was visiting my parents for Thanksgiving in November 2013, my mom asked if I was ready to write about Mace. I had published a children's cookbook three years before and had spent a lot of time promoting that book. I was ready for a new project. I took home with me some of Mace's

Mace in his "Hadassah" Jeep. "I never got mad at God.
I figured he made me so that's it," he once said.

photos and a few of the many articles written about him, figuring
I'd get a start.

A few days later, the strangest thing happened.

My mom forwarded me an email forwarded to her from
my grandmother's last living first cousin, Bill Sager, well into his
nineties at the time, but still in possession of his steel trap memory.
It seemed that Bill's great nephew, a distant cousin of mine named
Mike Sager, was trying to find out some information about Mace.
Sager was a writer, working on an article for *Esquire* about the
acclaimed dwarf actor Peter Dinklage. While writing his piece,
Sager remembered seeing photos of Cousin Mace and had some
questions about him.

Mike and I emailed and then spoke; I told him about the
Mace photos, and he offered me the amazing opportunity to work
together on this book. Maybe some people would call it coinci-
dence or providence, but I have another word for this kind of en-
ergetic, seemingly random connection: *amacing*.

Over the last two years, I've had the joy of speaking about Mace with many people: my mom and her first cousins David, Sue, Amy, Charles and Pamela; other cousins more removed like Howard Kerbel; and friends from Easton who knew Mace growing up, including Alan Kantor, Peter Cooper, Steve Lyons, Steve Glazier. All had their own unique take on Mace, and talking about him made them—and me—feel happy and connected to his considerable spirit.

In my research I was fortunate to discover a trove of articles written about Mace and his antics over the years. Grandma Min also kept a file of all of those interviews, so I had access to Mace's reflections and recollections about his life, told in his own words.

I also had my memory. My grandmother was an enthusiastic storyteller and I hungered for stories. Often as I was growing up, we sat together like magnets, and she transported me from my middle-class 1980s upbringing to her 1920s, first-generation American, waste-no-penny childhood.

The beauty of memory is its imperfection. I am sure many people who knew Mace will read this depiction of him and have other stories to tell about his life and his photos, how he built his business, or how he got away with one of his many charades.

That's fine, of course. Mace might have been small, but his story is quite larger than life, which is how he wanted it. More than anything, Mace lived his life in pursuit of one goal—to be special, not because of his deformity, but because of his contributions, good works, and daring spirit. His was a life well lived.

—Gabrielle Kaplan-Mayer

CELEBRITIES

With Harry James. The big band leader, James played trumpet
with Benny Goodman and later was the first to hire a young vocalist
named Frank Sinatra.

With Jane Russell (far right). One of Hollywood's sex symbols in the 1940s and 1950s, Russell played opposite Marilyn Monroe in *Gentlemen Prefer Blondes*. 1971.

With (left to right) Burgess Meredith, Anne Jackson and Edward G. Robinson. Meredith was an actor on both stage and screen—known more recently for his roles as the Penguin in the *Batman* television series and as Sylvester Stalone's trainer in *Rocky*. Jackson was an Obie-winning, Tony-nominated stage actress. Robinson, an actor during Hollywood's Golden Age, was known for playing gangsters and was given an Honorary Academy Award after his death in 1973. 1968.

With Jack Benny (right). The comedian got his start in vaudeville and radio and then transformed his TV variety show into the first sitcom.

With Danny Kaye. The popular actor/singer/dancer/comedian/television personality is best remembered for playing the title characters in *The Secret Life of Walter Mitty* and *Hans Christian Anderson*. 1971.

With Sammy Davis Jr. The iconic black, Jewish, and one-eyed member
of the Rat Pack was a singer, dancer, actor, and beloved personality.

With Isaac Stern (center). The renowned Jewish violinist played around
the globe but refused to perform in Germany. He mentored younger
musicians, including cellist Yo-Yo Ma and violinist Itzhak Perlman. 1976.

With Jack Gilford. The Broadway actor and film star was nominated for Tony Awards for his roles in *A Funny Thing Happened On The Way To The Forum* and *Cabaret*. He was blacklisted during the McCarthy era for his social activism.

With Richard Bernard "Red" Skelton. The comedic actor got his
start in the early days of radio and went on to host
"The Red Skelton Show" on TV for two decades. 1971.

With Ella Fitzgerald. Known as "The First Lady Of Song,"
the jazz singer won 13 Grammy awards and sold more than
40 million albums in her lifetime. 1973.

With Art Carney (center). The actor won six Emmy awards for playing
"Ed Norton" on the popular TV show *The Honeymooners*. 1972.

With Jackie Mason. Ordained as a rabbi, Mason left his synagogue
job to go into show biz, struck out on the Borsht Belt in the 1950s,
but hit it big on Broadway in the 1980s.

With Van Cliburn. One of the greatest pianists in the history of music,
the Lousiana-born Cliburn is best known for winning, at age 23,
the 1958 International Tchaikovsky Competition in Moscow. 1972.

With Molly Picon (front left). The darling of the Yiddish musical
theater, Picon performed on stage, film, radio, and television
in Europe, Israel, Africa, Australia, and the United States.

With Eydie Gorme (crouching, second from left) and Steve Lawrence (second from right). "Steve and Eydie" were a Grammy-winning husband and wife duo with musical hits in the 1950s, 1960s, and 1970s. 1972.

With Jan Peerce. A child of Polish immigrants, Peerce grew up
in a coldwater flat on the Lower East Side of New York City.
At 28 he debuted with the Radio City Music Hall Company and
made his opera debut six years later in Rigelleto. He would go on to
star on Broadway, in solo recitals, and as a recording artist. 1974.

With Mickey Rooney. A versatile performer, Rooney could sing,
dance, clown, and play various musical instruments, becoming
a celebrated character actor later in a career marked by precipitous
declines and raging comebacks. 1969.

With Henry Morgan, 1963. The satirist performed on radio
and TV but is best known for the 14 years he was a panelist
on *I've Got A Secret*.

With Milton Berle (center). The comedian, known as
"Uncle Miltie," was the first major TV star and the founder
of the Friars Club of Beverly Hills. 1976.

With Tom Jones. The Welsh pop singer, whose real name is
Sir Thomas Jones Woodward, is best known for his showmanship
and smooth baritone in such hits as "She's a Lady" and
"It's Not Unusual." He is still recording and performing. 1971.

With Dr. Jonas Salk (kneeling in suit). The son of Russian Jewish
immigrants and the first member of his family to attend college,
Salk went on to medical school and developed the vaccine for polio.

With Yehudi Menuhin. Considered one of the greatest violinists
of the twentieth century, Menuhin not only played classical music
but also played with jazz artists and recorded and played concerts
with sitarist Ravi Shankar.

THE LITTLE
GATE-CRASHER.

I n Phillipsburg, New Jersey, a factory town known for making pumps and rock drills for the private sector and the military, a nineteen-year-old Jewish boy named Moishe Bugen, the son of Eastern European immigrants who ran a corner grocery store, begged his older brother to put him on a bus to Chicago so he could see the boxer Joe Louis fight his first professional bout.

The year was 1934, and Louis was facing Jack Kracken, a boxer of Norwegian descent who was one of Chicago's top heavyweights at the time. Louis was a determined, dignified young man who'd come north with his family to escape the threat of the Ku Klux Klan in the rural Alabama town where he was born.

Louis had come to prominence as a lightweight fighter while he was still in high school, carrying his boxing gloves in a violin case so his mother wouldn't know what he was doing. Discovered by boxing promoter Julian Black, Louis fought in the amateur Golden Gloves' Open Division, winning the light heavyweight classification and also winning the Chicago Tournament of Champions. Now Black had set him up for his first professional bout against the heavyweight Kracken at the Bacon Casino on Chicago's South Side. According to sportswriters, Kracken, who had finished a tour of the Pacific Northwest undefeated the year before, was favored to make short work of the newcomer.

In school the teachers knew Moishe by his American name, Morris. All his friends and family called him Mace. From the time he was young, Mace was obsessed with sports, especially boxing. His older brother, Phil, a stolid and well-built football player who attended Lafayette College in Easton, Pennsylvania, knew that if he helped Mace, he'd have consequences to face. Their mother, Sarah Sager Bugen, was a force of nature, still fiercely protective of her nearly grown sons. She didn't care that Phil was a big shot football player admired by all the girls and beloved on campus; her displeasure would be considerable when she discovered what he'd done without her permission. But Phil could never say no to his little brother. And besides, Phil thought, maybe this kind of adventure was just the thing Mace needed.

When they arrived at the Greyhound station, Phil bought his nineteen-year-old brother a child's fare, usually applicable to kids twelve and under. Mace, who was 43 inches tall, winked at Phil; in the depths of the Great Depression, every penny counted.

The next morning, when the bus arrived at its destination, the driver couldn't help but notice a deep five-o'clock shadow on the face of his child fare. Unabashed, Mace gathered himself and left the bus. He might have been an achondroplastic dwarf— with an average size head and torso set on small, twisted legs—but that didn't mean he was an idiot or a pushover. In truth, he was smarter than most; over the years, he learned to effectively turn what society in those days called a *handicap* into a powerful tool he could use to his advantage.

Though he had never traveled anywhere without his parents and four siblings, Mace found his way through the bustling, crowded city of Chicago to the arena where the fight was to be held. He walked though the entrance, past the ticket takers. As usual, nobody asked him for a ticket. While people often stared, he'd noticed, they often shunned him as well, effectively treating him as if he was wasn't really there. If people were going to pre-tend to ignore him, Mace figured, he might as well take advantage, a small tax on their rudeness. Similarly, he strolled past the ush-ers and found himself a ringside seat, right next to Louis' corner.

The crowd was screaming as Kracken and Louis were brought into the ring. Moved by the excitement, the wonderful and heart-thumping perversity of his caper so far, Mace jumped out of his seat and climbed through the bottom ropes of the ring. Wearing his usual custom-made button-down shirt and knickers, he was about the height of an average four-year-old boy, and often was just as stubborn as one. With no care for consequences, he went right up to Louis and seized in his small hands Louis' giant brown leather gloves.

"I'm Mace Bugen," he declared. "I wanna wish ya some Jewish luck."

The crowd was cheering. The fight was about to begin. Louis, twenty years old and moments away from his first profes-sional boxing match, looked down at the odd little dwarf with the big smile standing before him.

"Man, I can use a little luck," Louis said.

At which point the referee forcibly removed Mace from the ring, to the delight of the crowd.

For some reason, Mace was not thrown out of the arena. He returned to his purloined seat, unmolested further.

The bell rang, the fight proceeded. Early in the going, Louis issued a left hook to the jaw that sent Kracken down for a count of nine. When Kracken regained his feet, Louis knocked him through the ropes and into the lap of Joe Triner, the chairman of the Illinois Athletic commission, a few seats away from Mace, who jumped up excitedly to watch. Kracken crawled back into the ring, but the referee stopped the bout, giving Louis his first profes-sional purse, $59.

Following the victory, there was pandemonium in the Bacon Casino, the usual jubilation and scrum of well-wishers. In the con-fusion, Mace followed Louis and his entourage back to Louis' locker room.

Removing his gloves, Louis hopped up onto the massage table for an alcohol rubdown, a common practice at the time. Laughing uproariously, one of his entourage reached down, picked up Mace by the armpits, and placed him on the table beside Louis.

"Maybe he really *is* a good luck charm," Louis laughed. Soon Louis would become known as The Brown Bomber, one of the biggest boxing champions of his time.

As photographers snapped pictures, Louis and Mace leaned together and smiled.

* * *

Mace's form of achondroplastic dwarfism is the most common type. According to the US National Library of Medicine, it occurs once in every fifteen thousand to forty thousand births. There are only about six thousand achondroplastic dwarfs born across the world each year. Dwarfism can be caused by two hundred distinct medical conditions; it's been found that achondroplastic dwarfism is a genetic condition, caused by a mutation on chromosome 4.

The history of dwarfs like Mace is mostly a depressing one. Being born in the early twentieth century in the United States didn't guarantee he would be treated with more humanity than the dwarfs who served as oddities and jesters in the fourteenth century—or even the dwarfs who would populate the classic movie *The Wizard of Oz*; the film's portrayal of little people, and the stories of off-set debauchery generated by the press, would cement the age-old image of dwarfs as a species apart.

Being born into the Bugen household meant that Mace was loved unconditionally. In good times and in lean, his family gave him every convenience he could possibly have. His mother sewed his clothes by hand.. Furniture in the home and at the store was adapted for his use. His father, Jacob "Jakie" Bugen, expected Mace to help out after school, just as his older brothers did. Though he knew he was out of place in the world, Mace was never out of place in the family. One thing could be said for Mace

Bugen: he had no lack of self-esteem. Deep down, Mace wanted to be considered special—only not for the reasons most people found so obvious.

Mace was my great-uncle; my mother was the daughter of his sister Minerva. When I was young, we saw quite a lot of Mace, visiting as families do. Often he would take us kids out for ice cream and other special treats; he was a doting great uncle in every way, always sending us birthday cards and treating each of us like we were somebody special. For understandable reasons, Mace was a magnet for children and teens; in later life he would become a counselor for a temple youth group. In children he found innocence and lack of judgement. In a way you could say that with kids, he saw eye-to-eye.

I was eleven years old when Mace died. I don't remember verbatim a lot of what he said. But I do very clearly remember him telling my sister and me about the roots of his personal philosophy.

"When I was a kid," he told us, "I'd ask myself, *Why is that guy on the football team? Why can't I be on the team? Why didn't God give me the height so I could be the hero?* Then at some point I figured out: I gotta do somethin' special to let 'em know I'm me."

Of course, Mace's encounter with Joe Louis, and the attendant buzz and celebrity that was created, turned out to be exactly what Mace had in mind. In a way, you could say that Mace, at a time before cell phones, preceding even Andy Warhol, was the world's first practitioner of the Celebrity Selfie—or maybe you could say more accurately that he was perhaps the world's first Selfie Photobomber. Over the next two decades, using his unique combination of guile, cunning, handicap, and entitlement, Mace engineered photos of himself with some of the biggest celebrities of his day, including Joe DiMaggio, "Babe" Ruth, Sammy Davis Jr, and Marilyn Monroe—the celluloid image of which has since disappeared. As the years passed, the collection of photos on a bulletin board in his office grew to include politicians, athletes, and Hollywood stars, among them: Edward G. Robinson, Jane Russell, Van Cliburn, Danny Kaye, George Gobel, Milton Berle, Jackie Mason, Tom Jones, Art Carney, Henry Morgan,

Kitty Carlisle, Burgess Meredith, "Red" Skeleton, Mickey Rooney, Anne Jackson, Joey Adams, Eddie Arnold, Lawrence Welk, Roberta Peters, Robert Merrill, Benny Goodman, Harry James, Martha Raye, Peggy Cass, Cesar Romero, and Victor Borge. Many of the photos survive and are included in this book. Many more were given away as gifts to his customers and friends.

Notably, there is one name missing list, the one who got away.

In Mace's recollections, there was only one VIP to ever turn him down.

Groucho Marx.

In a column dated September 28, 1955, Walter Winchell, the iconic syndicated gossip writer for the *New York Daily Mirror*, included this item in his roundup:

"The dwarf who crashes the gate at most major sports events (past the cops and attendants) is 'Mace' Bugen, an insurance and realty man of Phillipsburg, NJ. Thereafter, Mace was dubbed the "The Little Gate-Crasher."

* * *

The weekend after his trip to Chicago, Mace's antics in the ring with Louis made it into the weekly RKO newsreel that was shown before movies in every theater across the country, including the Chamber Street Theater in Phillipsburg.

Everyone in town—and millions across the world—saw Mace going though his hilarious and ballsy routine with the Brown Bomber. All the kids in school, all the factory workers from Ingersoll-Rand who'd stop by Bugen's Corner Store to get their lunchmeat on the way into the early shift, *everybody* in town was abuzz with questions. *How'd you get to Chicago, Macey? How'd you get your picture with Louis?* According to one high school teacher from Phillipsburg, on vacation in Norway at the time, Mace was even featured on the newsreel there! It was one of the biggest events to ever hit the tiny town, which was heretofore known mostly for being a place between places, a transportation hub between Pennsylvania's industrial Lehigh Valley and New York City.

Even though he was nineteen at the time, Mace was still in high school, repeating his senior year. For much of his school career, Mace was accompanied to classes by his sister, Minerva. Older by five years, and an excellent student, Minerva did Mace's homework, sat next to him in class, even helped during exams. Though everyone who knew Mace was aware that his intellect was sharp, he was treated by the school system generally as if his problem was more than just physical—because of his dwarfism, he was considered physically and mentally disabled.

During his junior year of high school, one teacher broke the pattern. Convinced that Mace was perfectly capable of doing the work himself, the teacher insisted that Mace take a test on *The Merchant of Venice* while sitting by her desk, without Minerva's help.

The next day, the teacher returned Mace's test with an F scrawled in red pen across the top. "You think because you are little, people are going to pity you," she said sternly. "You have to do your own homework. You're smart. There's no reason why you can't study."

In the face of this adversity, Mace was ready to quit school, but his mother wouldn't hear of it. "I don't care if it takes you a hundred years, you're going to graduate Phillipsburg High," Sarah Bugen insisted.

Mace finally graduated in June, 1935, at the age of twenty. Also in June of that year, a twenty-one year old Joe Louis defeated Primo Carnera in six breath-taking rounds to become the world champion, his first title.

* * *

When Mace announced his intention to learn to drive a car, no one in the family dared say no—stopping a determined Mace was impossible, as everyone knew.

An old Chevrolet Coupe was procured from a customer who owed a debt to the store. Harry Bugen, the eldest sibling, considered the most handy, was assigned the task of rigging the car so that Mace—with his congenitally short arms and legs—could reach the gas and brake pedals. Seeing him sitting in the seat, you might think he was a regular-sized young man. It was his short and twisted limbs that made things difficult for him. Today, many dwarfs have operations to straighten their legs, in order to make walking more comfortable and to ease the load on the spine.

On the appointed day, after much driving practice around town, brother Phil, always known for his charm, was charged with taking Mace to Trenton for the driver's exam. When they arrived, Phil made his brother stay put in the car while he went inside to talk to the people at the bureau. What transpired next is a secret Phil took with him to the grave. Did he grease the officer's palm? Did he win over the officer with his charm, carefully painting a picture of his unique and unfortunate brother waiting outside in the car with his heart set on getting a driver's license?

What we know for sure is that the officer got into the passenger seat beside Mace without blinking an eye and ordered the candidate to drive through a course of cones set up in the parking lot. As the story goes, Mace might have been a little nervous. The jury-rigged controls might have been a little hinky. And Mace might have driven a tad too fast and knocked down an orange cone or two.

Even so, he passed.

Of course, it was one thing for Sarah Bugen to agree to a driver's test. It was quite another when her precious Mace was to be driving all over the place by himself.

From the time he was born, Sarah accepted Mace's difference and only wanted him to succeed and have everything America offered to her other children. Sarah had immigrated from a *shtetl* in Lithuania, a Jewish ghetto in the old country, where the evil eye and other antiquated superstitions ruled. She was as religious and pious as her mother had been and her mother before her, but Sarah was also touched and inspired by the opportunities for learning America offered.

A take-charge parent, Sarah believed in putting extra effort toward creating an outcome desired. When Phil wanted to become a Boy Scout, for instance, Sarah didn't want him to eat nonkosher food, so she volunteered to be the cook for the troop. She packed up all five children; they slept in tents with the other Scouts at a wilderness campsite. Her food was so good the troop asked her to become its permanent cook for future camping trips.

Sarah insisted all of her five children do well in school, boys and girls. The eldest, Harry, studied business at New York University. Phil earned an athletic scholarship to Lafayette College. Minerva, who was singled out in high school for her dramatic talents, received private elocution lessons before being sent off to study theater at Emerson College in Boston. Though it was unheard of in the Bugen's circle of immigrant friends to pay for a daughter's higher education, particularly to study a field so "frivolous" as theater, the Bugens did so gladly, scraping together the funds from Sarah's savings—and taking loans from Sarah's wealthy brother-in-law, a businessman named Louis Malos. Later, the youngest daughter, Phyllis, would attend nursing school at the Jersey City Medical Center and earn an education degree from New Jersey State Teachers College.

When Mace received his driver's license, Sarah, in her typical fashion, wrote a letter to the US Army and requested a car of some sort that would be safe for her "handicapped" son to drive. He needed a vehicle, she wrote in her immigrant's hand, that was "that was up to military standards."

Unfortunately, the army was not willing to give a car to a civilian. So instead she went to the Ingersoll-Rand factory and hired an engineer-mechanic to custom-build a car for Mace, equipped with special brake and gas pedals. The little car looked kind of like a Jeep-knockoff. It provided Mace with an official air. He painted "US War Bonds" on the side and put a placard of a Jewish star in the front window, adding even more to his special status around town.

When Mace graduated from high school, his parents were prepared to send him on to college like the others. From an early age, Mace had insisted that the special clothes his mother would sew for him look like uniforms—a soldier, a fireman, a police officer. Even as she lovingly stitched every outfit, Sarah held the heartbreak that Mace could never grow up to do any of those jobs.

When Mace declared his interest in becoming a lawyer, Sarah called a family friend from the synagogue who was a partner at a big law firm. The friend obliged, as everyone did when Mrs. Bugen made a call, and scheduled an appointment for Mace to come visit the office.

Upon arrival, Mace shook the lawyer's hand and hoisted himself up into the leather armchair opposite the tall desk where the lawyer sat. The man took down a law book from a high shelf and opened it up to show Mace exactly what the letter of the law looked like.

Mace couldn't help noticing that the book looked huge—large and heavy and thick. "How many of these books do you have to study at law school?" he asked.

The lawyer gestured to his bookshelf, to the rows and rows and rows of thick leather-bound books.

Mace knew he could never manage to lug books that size around campus. He'd have to find another profession.

* * *

With his head for business and his way with people, Mace naturally stepped into the role of running the day-to-day operations at Bugen's Corner Market. Purveyors of canned goods, fresh fruits, vegetables, and an extensive selection of meats, the store was located on Marshall Street. Mace had enjoyed working in the store since he was a boy; over the years, he learned to maneuver around his physical disadvantages. If a customer requested sliced lunch meat, for instance, Mace would invite the customer to take the meat out of the cooler him or herself and to place it on the slicer—giving the transaction a more customized feel. (Mace would stand on a box and crank the lever to slice the meat.) To grab cans from top shelves, Mace employed a store-bought "reacher." In time he also showed a gift for accounting. He started keeping records of money owed by customers to whom his father often gave easy—and sometimes uncollectable—credit. Mace wasn't as soft about collecting as his father was. He'd cut off credit until bills were paid. Under his management, Bugen's Corner Market began making greater profits.

As the war years passed and veterans were coming home to begin life anew and start families, Mace noticed an opportunity—buying, fixing up, and selling older properties in the rougher neighborhoods of Phillipsburg and Easton.

The two small towns, set on opposite sides of the Delaware River, were connected by the Bushkill Street Bridge (now the Easton-Phillipsburg Toll Bridge), built in 1938. At the time it was created, the four-lane span was the country's largest steel truss bridge. Though it connected cities in two different states—Easton in Pennsylvania and Phillipsburg in New Jersey—the bridge created a sort of small Eastern version of Minnesota's Twin Cities; the two localities became symbiotic. Easton was the richer side, the seat of Northampton County and the home of Lafayette College. Phillipsburg was smaller, grittier, and more working class, the home of the Ingersoll-Rand factory, which manufactured pumps and rock drills for military and industrial uses. Both towns had a large stock of dilapidated houses. Mace worked both sides of the bridge to scoop up the cheapest properties he could find for easy renovation and resale.

To fix up the houses, Mace hired returning veterans to do roofing, plumbing, and general construction, paying a few dollars a day plus all the groceries they wanted from the store. Renters were not a problem. The houses filled quickly; with the proceeds, Mace bought more properties. On the first of every month, Mace went personally to all the locations to collect rent. Those who couldn't pay were given a few months grace—after that, they were out.

Only five years out of high school, Mace's business was booming. Along the way, to cut down expenses and to take advantage of further opportunities, Mace picked up a real estate license and then became a notary. Later he opened an insurance firm. In time he bought an office building on Warren Street in Phillipsburg to house his enterprises, which together comprised a clever kind of one-stop shopping for homes and apartments.

POLITICIANS

With New York Mayor Fiorello La Guardia. The 99th mayor of NYC,
La Guardia served three terms, defeated the Tammany Hall political
machine, and crossed party lines to become a New Deal Republican. 1946.

With Barry Goldwater. The five-term US senator from Arizona
was the Republican Party's nominee for president in the
1964 election. He is credited for sparking the resurgence of
the American conservative political movement in the 1960s.

With Abba Eban. The Israeli diplomat Eban served as Israel's
minister for foreign affairs and deputy prime minister. He was also
an ambassador to the United States and to the United Nations.

With Hubert H. Humphrey. The two-term US senator from
Minnesota served as the 38th vice president of the United States
under President Lyndon B. Johnson from 1965 to 1969.
He was the nominee of the Democratic Party in the 1968 presiden-
tial election, losing to the Republican nominee, Richard Nixon.

With Richard Nixon. After defeating Humphrey, Nixon became
the 37th president of the United States. He served from 1969 to
1974, when he became the only U.S. president to resign the office.
"I am not a crook," he said. 1969.

During the war, Mace had a number of women friends with whom he'd spend time, many of them lonely girls pining for fiancés serving overseas. Mace would take them to movies, to the soda fountain, or to the ice cream shop. Once GI boyfriends began arriving home, however, his social life was not as active.

In 1937, sister Minerva married a German Jewish refugee named Georg Auerbach, who became Mace's close friend and confidant. Minerva worried about Mace being lonely. At one point Minerva, through some New York cousins, contacted a female dwarf who lived in that city. A double date to a Broadway show was arranged.

Encountered in the theater lobby, Mace's date was, like himself, an achondroplastic dwarf—a pretty woman with a characteristically "normal" sized head and torso and short arms and legs. She smiled at Mace and gave Minerva a hug. Minerva was pleased and hopeful.

As the foursome proceeded down the long aisle to their seats near the front, Mace couldn't help but notice the stares and comments being aimed their way. Mortified, the usually talkative Mace was dumbstruck. At intermission, when Georg suggested the foursome visit the bar, thinking a small libation would lighten the mood, Mace refused to budge from his seat.

In the car on the way home, Mace told Minerva he would never go out with another dwarf again. He was miserable, he said. Everyone in the theater was gawking at them. It was like a freak show. Didn't she hear the laughter?

Minerva had never seen Mace in this state before. Usually he seemed so pleased with himself, so confident. At times, it even seemed he carried with him an air of superiority, as if he was actually better than all the "norms." Certainly he used his size to his advantage in business. People felt uncomfortable haggling prices with a dwarf, and he knew it. He often settled on higher rents or sales prices for properties for just this reason. In the past, Minerva had never seen Mace give any signs that he was angry or resentful about his differences. But this time he told her flat out: Walking down that theater aisle as part of a dwarf couple had been the most humiliating event of his entire life. Always a gentleman, he went on to tell his sister that he'd felt even worse about the humiliation his date must have felt. Never again, he vowed, would he date another "little person."

Given the social mores in the 1940s and 1950s, when dating out of one's race was considered a taboo—and illegal in many states—it was unlikely that Mace would find a woman of more normal height to date or marry. With his options limited, Mace created for himself a network of friends, most of them married couples. Often he'd take a married woman friend on the train the short distance to New York to the Metropolitan Opera or to see a Broadway show; in most cases, their husbands didn't care to go anyway. Over time, he became a perfect third wheel. Mace always chose attractive women to befriend; he often said he liked being seen with a beautiful woman on his arm. He might have been a dwarf, but he was still a man.

Meanwhile, to satisfy his more private needs, Mace became well known among the prostitutes of Easton-Phillipsburg. "If I wanted somethin', I'd spend ten dollars," he'd later explain.

In general, Mace didn't like to be alone, and he didn't like having idle time.

Part of every day was spent in his office on Warren Street, which housed his insurance/real estate/notary business. It wasn't fancy—just a desk and chair for Mace and a few chairs for his customers. On the wall was a bulletin board, where he would pin up photos from the celebrities he had met. Often, townspeople would drop in to see Mace's latest photos and walk out with a new life insurance policy.

The rest of his days were filled with things to do and people to see. He did a lot of charity work for Jewish causes, visited old folks in the retirement home. He kept track of his schedule on a thick white tablet of paper with the words, "From the Desk of Morris 'Mace' Bugen," printed at the top.

Mace prided himself on his frugality. A child of the Depression, he made every penny count. On Sunday mornings, he went to Joe's Sandwich shop, helped himself to a Sunday newspaper, and spread it out on the floor to read. When he finished, he'd fold it back up and replace it in the stand, preferring not to waste his money.

Even after his businesses were well established, Mace spent a lot of time at Bugen's Corner Market, looking after the books and making sure the orders had been placed and the stock clerks had filled the shelves, and making sure the needs of his aging parents were being met, shuttling them back and forth from pinochle and bridge games, to doctors' appointments, to shul, and to family occasions. Mace devoted a lot of his time to helping his mother with her charitable pursuits through Hadassah, an organization that began as a small mission to provide emergency care to infants and mothers in prestate Israel that has since flourished as a Jewish charity. Chief among Mace's activities was collecting rummage that Sarah would sell to support refugees settling in Israel.

Meanwhile, Mace became a fixture around the community. For more than thirty years, he never missed an athletic contest—baseball, football, basketball—between rival high schools in Easton and Phillipsburg. For twenty years, Mace was the official timekeeper for league basketball games at the Young Men's Hebrew Association—though it was well known that if the home team was losing, five minutes left on the clock could sometimes stretch to fifteen . . . nobody was going to argue with the dwarf.

As his siblings had kids of their own, Mace also made time for weekly dates with his seven nieces and nephews—everyone's favorite outings were to Calliope's Sweet Shop and Rapp's Ice Cream Fountain. Likewise, Mace didn't miss a special event—if there was a bar mitzvah or a wedding going on in the vicinity, you'd find him on the guest list.

An observant Jew, Mace was a regular at the little shul in Easton, Bnai Abraham, where he went weekly to observe the Sabbath. Every December, he drove a car full of fellow shul members to New York City for the annual Hanukkah ball to benefit Israel Bonds; likewise, he patronized the annual balls in Philadelphia. As time went by, Mace bought a new Jeep CJ, one of the first consumer models of the Willys MB combat trucks that became known during WWII as Jeeps. Eventually he would customize his Jeep with a Jewish theme, painting it blue and white, the colors of the Israeli flag, and covering the vehicle in Jewish stars. In the surrounding Lehigh Valley, where only 2 percent of the population was Jewish, he was like a one-man Jewish pride parade, albeit a somewhat freakish one, by the standards of any age. "If you went to something—a service, a concert, any event in the Jewish community—and Mace wasn't there, you were like, 'Where's Mace?' " remembers an Easton friend from those years.

In 1946, at age thirty-one, Mace ran for the office of town commissioner of Phillipsburg. His slogan: "I'm for the Little Guy."

Though he lost the election by a wide margin, by the time it was over, everyone in the Lehigh Valley knew his name.

* * *

After meeting Joe Louis, Mace began carrying a camera with him everywhere he went.

The type and model of camera he used varied over the years—only one photo shows him actually holding a camera, in that case it appears to be a classic Kodak Instamatic, flash cube affixed. Technically, none of the photos are great, except for the few grin-and-grabs that were taken at events by official photographers. Most of the shots in his gallery were blurry or ill-framed, having been taken in a rush by the nearest accomplice, often a stranger. For many years, Mace carried his camera in a woman's cosmetic bag, smaller and less heavy than a traditional camera case. In short order the red leather bag became part of Mace's trademark. "If you see Mace with that red bag, you know you're in trouble," Minerva would say, laughing with an almost parental pride. Of all the kids, she knew Mace best; she'd accompanied him to school every day for years. In this weird hobby of his, she saw the gathering strength of his self esteem. Like everyone in their nuclear family, she just wanted Mace to feel comfortable in his own skin.

Over time and through practice, Mace developed a series of strategies for obtaining his photos.

When his quarry was not to be found inside the Lehigh Valley, where his reputation proceeded him and doors swung, Mace usually masqueraded as a journalist. Waving his camera, talking fast, he would mumble something about being a reporter "for a paper in Jersey." As usual, Mace's physical difference would tend to dumbfound anyone he met. Nobody was ever quite sure how to act at first. As he became older, Mace became more and more comfortable in his own skin; in a way, he learned to make his difference into an advantage—he took great pleasure in gaming the Norms. It was as much a part of the game as the meeting and the photo. In later years, after he was dead, my sister and I began to think of Mace's abilities to make people bend to his will as his Jedi mind trick, after the mind control techniques used in the *Star Wars* movie franchise. In sum, Mace had this curious talent for making people enable him, especially when he was acting like he was where he belonged. Some would call his the work of a man on a mission. Some would call it a talent for con. I believe Mace thought of it as a little bit sport, a little bit entitlement. Long before the The Americans with Disabilities Act of 1990 brought accommodations of all kinds, Mace evened the playing field in his own way.

At newsworthy events, Mace would insinuate himself in front of the scrum of bona fide photographers and journalists and wait around patiently with the others for the arrival of the dignitary.

When the celeb got out of the car or stepped onto the red carpet, flashbulbs would begin to pop.

That would be Mace's cue. He'd hand his camera to a friend or a startled bystander and then rush forward with all the quickness his crippled body could command. Reaching the target of the evening—in one case, it was Richard Nixon—he'd stretch out his hand to shake, and meanwhile bellow to his accomplice:

"Quick, buddy, take the picture!"

(Which might be the reason why, in so many of the photos that have been recovered, Mace seems to be shouting at his quarry. In nearly all the photos, there is a somewhat wild look in Mace's eyes. The celebrities tend to look a little bit stunned.)

For a short burst of time—a period perhaps as long as the retinal afterburn from his camera flash—everything in the vicinity around Mace and the celebrity would freeze: the burly security men, the jostling members of the press, the fans and bystanders, all of them wondering . . . *What is that dwarf doing?*

* * *

In July 1950, two years after Israel had become a state, Mace made his first trip to the Holy Land with a tour group of Jewish American businessmen. In Tel Aviv, in the lobby of the King David Hotel where he was staying, he met a young Israeli woman; he invited her to coffee and she accepted. When they were finished, she in turn invited Mace to go with her to the Knesset, the Israeli Parliament. Prime Minister David Ben-Gurion was about to give a speech.

In a time before metal detectors, the security officers at the Israeli house of government asked Mace about the contents of his red cosmetic bag. Mace explained he used it as seat cushion and was allowed to pass. Sent to the third-floor gallery, Mace complained to his companion that he couldn't see the proceedings below. "Could we go down to the main floor?" he asked. "I'm sure nobody will mind."

The guard on the door allowed them to pass. Ben-Gurion was already on the dais speaking.

The next morning, July 8, 1950, the Hebrew daily newspaper, *Ma'ariv* published a story headlined "Midget Invades Knesset. An English translation appears below:

> *The sensation of yesterday evening's Knesset session occurred during the discussion of the profiteering issue. All of a sudden a midget "invaded' the hall. He ran almost to the center of the hall where the session was taking place; he jumped on top of an empty chair which belonged to a Mapai delegate and with a flash-bulb*

camera he snapped a picture of the dais including the head of state. Then with miraculous speed, he slipped away, actually running between the legs of the ushers.

The flash-bulb of this strange midget caused a great shock in the Knesset. A reporter quickly followed on the heels of the invading photographer and succeeded in catching him on the steps before the exit and also to interview him. What emerged is that this midget is a tourist from America. His name is Mace Bugen, 35 years of age, and as he himself remarked he is 43 centimeters tall and weighs 47 kilos. In New Jersey where he has a brokerage agency, he has a father, mother, two brothers and two sisters—all of whom are of normal height. He arrived in Israel a few days ago with a group of 28 Zionist businessmen.

Bugen is a photography fan and he showed us newspaper clippings that he has photographed many noted celebrities among them; President Truman, Generals Eisenhower and Marshall, O'dwyer, Mayor of New York, the prizefighters Dempsey, Joe Louis, Baer, movie stars, artists, etc.

When I pointed out to him that it is forbidden to take pictures in the Kenesset at the time of their session, he answered me winking, as a wise-guy, "That's just what I enjoy."

* * *

Mace didn't only steal photos—occasionally his quarry would befriend him and he'd share a deeper experience. His ongoing friendship with Joe Louis was well documented. In 1968, when Richard Nixon was out campaigning against Lyndon Johnson, Mace spent a few quiet moments in conversation with the future US president. Another night, at an Israeli Bonds fund-raiser, Mace befriended Sammy Davis Jr., the well-known African-American entertainer who'd converted to Judaism. Davis brought Mace up on stage with him and enlisted his enthusiasm in hawking bonds for the Jewish state.

After an uninvited visit to the dressing room of Mollie Picon, one of the biggest stars of the Yiddish theater in America, Mace charmed the actress with his command of Yiddish. Over the years they became pen pals; Mace visited Picon whenever she came to New York to perform. Encountering operatic tenor Jan Peerce at the Hotel Easton, Mace asked him, "Who are you eating breakfast with tomorrow?" The photo from the next morning shows them at breakfast together, along with Peerce's wife.

As Mace aged, he began to cut back his daily workload. A factor was the deteriorating state of his spine, which made it more difficult to walk. He began to spend more time at his synagogue, Bnai Abraham, in Easton. A tireless volunteer and contributor to Jewish causes, Mace occasionally helped the rabbi lead religious services. He also worked closely with a youth program that aimed to keep teens connected to the temple after bar mitzvah. The Tallis and Tefillin Club met every Sunday morning for prayers, bagels and lox, and the occasional outing. Generally, that's where Mace came in.

As it turned out, like the Lost Boys following a dwarf Peter Pan, the kids were willing and enthusiastic accomplices in Mace's photo gathering schemes. He drove them around town in his Jeep; for longer trips he drove his specially rigged Studebaker; sometimes he crammed as many as seven kids into the roomy car. By this time, Mace often used a wheelchair to get around; there was ample room room in the trunk. Often he'd drive the kids to Philadelphia or New York for a baseball game. One time he handed out dark glasses to all the boys and had them push him to the gate, where he explained to the ticket taker that his charges were from a home for blind orphans. In no time they were whisked to the pricey seats.

On one occasion Mace took a crowd of kids to see the New York Knicks play the Philadelphia 76ers at the Palestra Arena at the University of Pennsylvania, a can't-miss National

Basketball League game, featuring Walt Frazier versus Julius "Dr. J" Erving.

As usual, Mace was given a great seat courtside. The boys, under the premise that they were orphans, were given seats several rows back.

During the game, a fight broke out.

In his 1970 book *Clyde*, Frazier describes what happened next:

"I remember one close game in the Palestra, which is a dump, with the crowd too close to the court. We had the lead and one of the refs made a call that the fans protested. Some guy took off across the floor after the official. The ref tried to have him thrown out of the game, but I guess he was a season ticket-holder, so they put him in a seat by Philly's bench. Then a second guy runs onto the court and starts kicking the ref in the leg and the ref looks around and doesn't see anybody because the guy is a midget! They had to drag the midget off the floor, but I don't think he got tossed out either."

Some years after the incident, Mace would talk his way into the Knick's dressing room and Frazier would recognize him. The resulting photo is part of his trove.

One of Mace's frequently retold stories involved meeting Muhammad Ali in 1968, the year after the fighter had infamously refused to serve in the US military during the Vietnam War. Ali had come to speak at Muhlenberg College in Allentown, and Mace, along with some of the boys from the T&T club, had road-tripped to see him. As soon as Ali began speaking, a fight broke out between war supporters and protestors. People started flooding toward the stage. Ali was hustled out the back door.

As he was getting into the car, Ali felt a tug at his pants leg. It was Mace.

There might have been a near-riot going on, but Mace got his picture.

A few years later, when Ali returned to boxing, word got out that he was training in Deer Lake, Pennsylvania, just forty-five minutes outside of Easton. The nation remained divided about the Vietnam war. Ali was still under intense media scrutiny and continued to be a polarizing figure. To train for his next bout, Ali sought the seclusion of the remote coal mining community, where he built a professional boxing ring and set to work with his trainers.

Mace loaded the boys into his car and took off, circling country roads around Deer Lake until they stumbled upon Ali's unmarked training camp. Though it was still early when Mace and crew arrived, he waved his cane in the air like a scepter and demanded that the security guards go wake the champ . . . so he could meet the poor orphan boys he'd brought.

As the story goes, all the commotion woke Ali, who came outside in his bathrobe and recognized Mace from their previous meeting. Ali brought Mace and the boys inside and ordered his cook to make them breakfast—no doubt some non-kosher bacon was involved. Then Ali personally gave the group a tour of his training camp; they watched him spar with an unknown young boxer named Larry Holmes, who would later go on to become heavyweight champion and defeat Ali. Of course, Mace would pose with him, too.

* * *

After my great-grandparents died in the early 1960s, Mace sold the grocery store. His sister Minerva—my Grandma Min—convinced Mace to move across the river to Easton to live with her.

Stubborn, creative and fiercely protective of Mace, much like her mother, Minerva worked with an architect to design an addition onto her house that would serve as a private apartment for Mace. Everything was custom-built to scale. There were extra-low counters in the kitchen and bath, a small dining table, a small desk and small chairs, a small bed and dresser, a small bathroom. Also, Mace's apartment had its own entrance from the rear, so he could come and go as he pleased. He parked his Studebaker in the garage; there was a spot in the adjoining alley for his Jeep.

I was born in 1971. By the time I was old enough to get to know Mace, his gate-crashing days were over. But Mace was a fixture in our childhood. Our mother, Lynn Auerbach-Kaplan, was Minerva's daughter with Georg Auerbach. When we were young, she would frequently bring us to visit. Mace would let us girls take over his apartment, which seemed like the greatest doll house every built. We played in there for hours. Sometimes Mace would let us serve him tea.

After Georg died, in 1977, at the age of sixty-five, Mace moved into a small apartment in Phillipsburg. Minerva reconverted Mace's apartment and rented it out to graduate students attending nearby Lafayette College.

In 1980, Mace had a stroke. Providentially, he was found on the floor of his apartment by my cousin Charlie, who regularly stopped by to check on him. The stroke left Mace unable to walk; his speech thereafter was slightly slurred. For the next two years, until his death in October 1982, Mace lived in a nursing home in Easton. It was a place he knew well: During his younger days, he'd made it a practice to visit residents there every Saturday.

* * *

There's another story my grandmother Minerva used to tell me; I think of it a lot.

It is 1917 and Minerva is four years old. She is chasing after her mother, Sarah, who is running up the stairs to catch the train from Phillipsburg to New York City. Minerva has never been on a train before. Her job is to carry a bag of oranges. Her mother lugs a heavier bag with a kosher lunch. Strapped to her back is a home-made child-carrier, secured with a wooden board and canvas straps. Inside the carrier is her fourth child, two years old. His head is clearly larger than the rest of his body. A local doctor in Phillipsburg had pronounced him a dwarf. It was a permanent condition, the doctor said. There was nothing to be done.

But Sarah is stubborn. She wants a second opinion. Through her circle of Russian Jewish immigrant cousins, she has found an orthopedic specialist in Manhattan. As she hustles up the steps to the train platform in her usual no-nonsense manner, she is carrying not only her child and the food she has packed for later, but also all of her hopes that this doctor, a New York big shot, will have some way to help her baby. The train whistle blows.

Trying to keep up, Minerva drops the bag of oranges and they spill, scattering, rolling one by one down the stairs. For a moment she freezes, unsure whether to chase the oranges or to keep after her mother and brother, the baby Mace.

Whenever Grandma Min told me this story, it always was my custom to interrupt at this point. "Did you get the oranges?" I'd ask anxiously. "Did you get on the train?"

Yes, she would tell me, a kind person helped her gather the oranges. She'd run her fastest and managed somehow to find her mother just as as the train doors closed.

I never asked her about the train ride home, about what she remembered from being at the doctor's office, or about her mother's grief when the specialist told her that nothing could be done to make her baby brother any different than he was.

I do know, however, that Mace made the most of every moment of his life, and that the evidence of his spirit has been left behind in his photos, a fitting tribute to the Little Gate-Crasher, a man who learned to turn his disadvantages into strengths.

As Mace himself once told me, *"I never got mad at God. I figured he made me so that's it."*

MACE'S LIFE

"MACE" BUGEN
● NOTARY PUBLIC ●
REAR
326 WARREN STREET
PHILLIPSBURG N. J. 08865

CAN BE REACHED BY PHONE

(201) 454 8290

BEFORE 9 AM OR AFTER 10 PM

An early business card.

At Bugen's Corner Market, age 15. 1930.

His first vehicle.

His "Hadassah" Jeep.

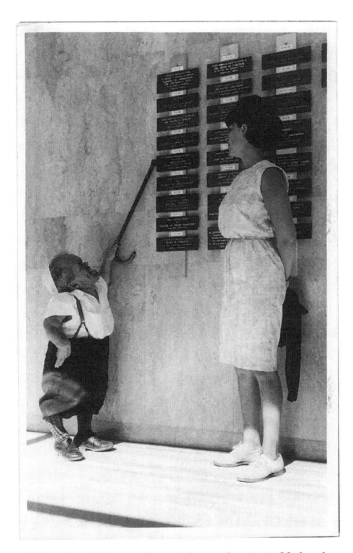

In Israel, pointing to a plaque in honor of service to Hadassah
by his mother, Sarah Sager Bugen.

The stool he took to sporting events.

His "Hadassah" Jeep.

With the author's parents.

The author, left, with her siblings, Julie, center and Jon,
and her grandmother, Minerva Bugen Auerbach. 1975.

Mace's apartment. 1968.

Mace's apartment. 1968.

Mace's apartment. 1968.

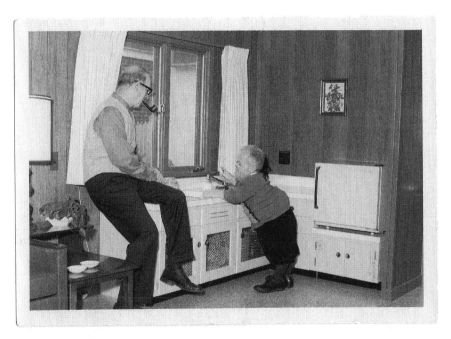

With his brother-in-law Georg Auerbach. 1968.

Working out at the gym at the Easton YMHA.

A family celebration. First row: Minerva Auerbach (Mace's sister, the author's maternal grandmother), Julie Kaplan (author's sister), Mace, the author, Georg Auerbach (Minerva's husband).
Top row: Bea Kaplan (the author's paternal grandmother), Steve Kaplan (the author's father), Lynn Auerbach-Kaplan (the author's mother), Joe Kaplan (the author's paternal grandfather.)

The author and her sister having ice cream with family friends,
Mace's treat.

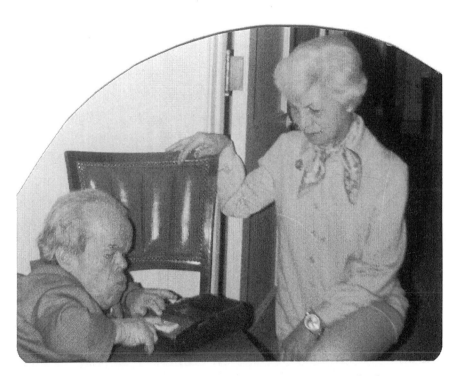

With Minerva Auerbach. Mace also enjoyed interviewing family
members and friends on his portable tape recorder.

Outside his office.

Deplaning in Israel. 1950.

ABOUT THE AUTHOR

Gabrielle Kaplan-Mayer is a freelance writer and educator based in Philadelphia. She directs "Whole Community Inclusion" at Jewish Learning Venture. Her recent books include *The Creative Jewish Wedding Book* and *The Kitchen Classroom*. She is a featured blogger for *Newsworks Philly Parenting* and writes for and edits *The New Normal: Blogging Disability*. Her work has appeared in *The New York Jewish Week*, *The Jewish Exponent* and Kveller.com.

ABOUT THE PUBLISHER

The Sager Group was founded in 1984. In 2012 it was chartered as a multi-media artists' and writers' consortium, with the intent of empowering those who make art—an umbrella beneath which makers can pursue, and profit from, their craft directly, without gatekeepers. TSG publishes eBooks and paper books; manages musical acts and produces live shows; ministers to artists and provides modest grants; and produces documentary, feature and web-based films. By harnessing the means of production, The Sager Group helps artists help themselves. For more information, please see www.TheSagerGroup.Net.

Made in the USA
Charleston, SC
16 February 2017